SEA
SQUARES

JOY N. HULME

— Illustrated by —

CAROL SCHWARTZ

Hyperion Paperbacks for Children
New York

Printed in the United States of America.
For more information address Hyperion Books for Children,
114 Fifth Avenue, New York, New York 10011.
First Hyperion Paperback edition: September 1993

10

Library of Congress Cataloging-in-Publication Data
Hulme, Joy N.
Sea squares / by Joy N. Hulme; illustrated by Carol Schwartz. — 1st ed.
p.   cm.
Summary: Rhyming text and illustrations of such sea animals as
whales, gulls, clown fish, and seals provide opportunities to practice
counting and squaring numbers from one to ten.
ISBN: 1-56282-079-6 (trade) / 1-56282-080-X (lib. bdg.)
1-56282-520-8 (pbk.)
1. Counting—Juvenile literature. 2. Multiplication—Juvenile literature.
3. Marine fauna—Juvenile literature. [1. Counting. 2. Multiplication.
3. Marine animals.] I. Schwartz, Carol, ill. II. Title.
QA113.H85 1991 513.5'5—dc20 [E] 91-71381 CIP AC

Carol Schwartz's illustrations are done in Designer's Gouache
on Strathmore 3-ply bristol. To achieve certain textures,
a combination of airbrushing and brush technique is used.

The text for this book is set in
22 pt. ITC Usherwood Book.

SEA
SQUARES

For all my children and grandchildren,
who love nimble numbers.

—J.H.

For Bob, Zachary, and Allison
—C.S.

Come with me to the side of the sea,
Where the ocean meets the shore.
We'll count some creatures that crawl and creep
Or grow on the ocean floor.
Some flop, some dive, some swim and swish,
Some fly where the breakers roar.

One one-ton whale, with one waterspout,
And one strong tail to push him about.

Can you count *1* spout, *1* whale,

And *1* strong tail?

Two two-eyed gulls, with two wide wings,
Shrieking and swooping and pecking up things.

2 white gulls, with *2* eyes each,
Have *4* bright eyes to watch the beach.

Three three-striped clown fish, black and white and red,
Nesting in anemones' spiny ocean bed.

3 clowns with frowny faces
Have 9 stripes in fishy places.

Four slippery seals, with four flippers each,
Swooping in the surf and flopping on the beach.

4 seals are quite complete,

With *16* flippery feet.

Five five-feathered sea lilies, waving fringy stalks,
Growing on the ocean floor, clinging to the rocks.

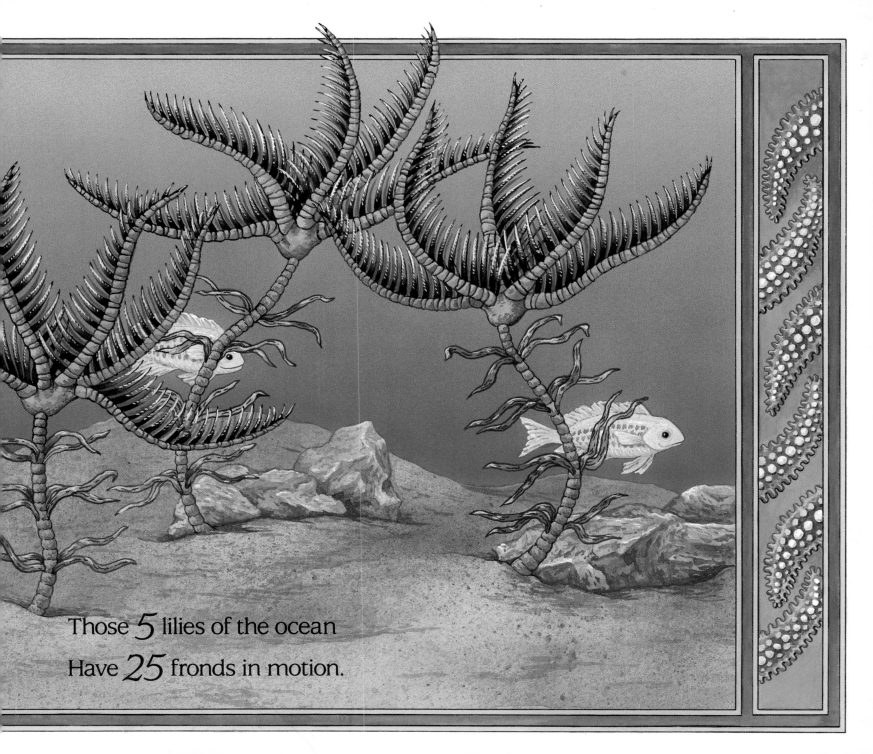

Those 5 lilies of the ocean
Have 25 fronds in motion.

Six six-pointed sea stars, with rays all around,
Turning seaside somersaults on the sandy ground.

That's only 6 sea stars sprawling,

But 36 arms are crawling.

Seven heavy pelicans diving for their dinner;
Seven fish in every pouch can never make them thinner.

7 pouchy pelicans
Gulp 49 fish with fins.

Eight eight-legged octopuses kicking in the ocean,
Stirring up the currents in a watery commotion.

8 "octos" on the ocean floor

Have scrambled legs, *64*.

Nine bottom-walking tubfish catching clams to munch;
Nine slurped up in every bite will make a tasty lunch.

9 tubfish have a treat

Of *81* clams to eat.

Ten squirmy squids squirting ten inky trails,
Pulling ten tentacles like ten wagging tails.

When *10* squids retreat so fast,
100 tails go swishing past.

It's always fun beside the sea,
Along the sandy shore,
To square the numbers of seals and such
Where the ocean breakers roar.
Why don't we stay for another day,
Or two, or three or four,
To count amounts, then square the counts
And tally up the score?

Some whales are the largest animals that have ever lived on Earth. Blue whales can be more than 100 feet long and weigh as much as 150 tons (50 times as much as an elephant). A *one-ton* whale, such as the beluga, is a small one. Because whales are mammals, not fish, they must hold their breath when they are underwater. When a whale rises to the surface to breathe, it exhales moist air in a "spout" through nostrils that are found on top of its head or at the end of its snout. Whales give birth to live young and nurse them with milk, as do land mammals.

Sea gulls are water birds. They are good swimmers but not very graceful in flight. They devour fish and other water animals as well as any kind of food or garbage that floats. Gulls swoop down and pick up edible tidbits from the water surface with their strong, hooked beaks.

Clown fish and sea anemones live together so they can be useful to each other. The anemones provide a thick, fringed fortress that hides the fish and protects them from their enemies. In exchange, the fish attract sea creatures that become food for both. Predators chase the colorful fish, expecting to catch a good meal. Instead, the clown fish lead them into a tangled trap where they are stung by poisoned, barbed threads shot from the waving tentacles of the anemone. The paralyzed predators become the dinner instead of the diner.

Eared, or fur, seals have long flippers that enable them to move quickly on land as well as in the water. Seal babies—or pups, as they are called—cannot swim, so they are always born on land. Fur seals are very noisy, especially when large numbers gather at breeding time. The bulls bark, roar, and fight savagely to claim their territory and protect their mates. The cows snarl and snap at one another. Even the pups howl, bleat, and squall for their mothers. What sounds like bickering and quarreling with one another is the pups' way of expressing themselves.

Although sea lilies, or feather stars, look like flowers, they are really ocean-floor animals that use their sticky, fringed fronds to catch food as it floats by.

Sea stars, or starfish, come in many starry shapes and sizes. Most have five arms around a central body disk, but some have six or more rays, and sun stars may have nine, ten, or eleven rays. If any of the arms is broken off, a new one will grow by a

process called regeneration. Even a small piece from a damaged sea star can grow into a complete new animal. To eat, sea stars wrap themselves around clams, oysters, or mussels and pull steadily with their sucking disks until they finally force the strong muscles that hold the shells together to relax. Pulling the shells apart slightly, the sea stars push their stomachs inside and digest the soft bodies.

Pelicans are the world's largest web-footed birds. They are swift swimmers and strong, graceful fliers but very awkward on land. They use their lower bills as scoops to catch small fish. Young pelicans feed by putting their heads deep into their parents' pouches to eat partly digested food. Contrary to popular belief, these birds do not store fish in their pouches.

Octopuses have eight tentacles around a mouth with horny jaws. Each snakelike arm has two rows of sucking disks that are used to grab fish, crabs, and lobsters and sweep them into the mouth. Usually the octopus crawls along the ocean floor and climbs over rocks using its sucker disks, but if in danger, it has a quicker method of moving. The octopus has a funnellike opening called a siphon situated just below its head. The octopus draws water into its body, then shoots the water out through its siphon. The sudden force propels the animal backward like a rocket. At the same time, the octopus can squirt a dark cloud of fluid through the siphon that hides it from its enemies.

Tubfish belong to the colorful sea robin fish family. Using their large, fanlike lower fins, they "walk" along the ocean floor. Sea robins also "sing" and can be very noisy. They eat small crustaceans (such as shrimps and crabs) and mollusks (such as clams and snails) and are found along African and European coasts.

Squids have long, spindle-shaped bodies with two flat tail fins on the pointed end and ten dangling appendages around a mouth on the other. Two of these arms are longer than the others, but all the arms are used to grab and hold the fish that squids catch and eat. Squids swim, tail end first, by filling cavities in their bodies with water and then forcing it rapidly out through a funnel. The sudden jet of water shoots the animal backward. To hide themselves, squids can change colors to match the background or squirt a dark camouflage fluid behind them as they flee from enemies.